DECLARATION AND ADDRESS

By THOMAS CAMPBELL

WITH AN INTRODUCTION BY
WILLIAM ROBINSON, M.A., B.SC., D.D., S.T.D.
Professor of Christian Doctrine and Theology
The School of Religion, Butler University
Indianapolis, U.S.A.

First Printing . 1951
Second Printing 1955

THE BEREAN PRESS
BRIGHTON ROAD
BIRMINGHAM

MADE AND PRINTED IN GREAT BRITAIN BY
WILLIAM CLOWES AND SONS LIMITED LONDON AND BECCLES
1*s.* 6*d.* (U.S.A. 30 cents)
Issued under the auspices of the James Donald Tract Fund

INTRODUCTION

This document, issued in 1809, coming from what was then called 'The New World', is a classic amongst the world's documents on Christian Unity. It forms one of the basic documents of the people variously known as 'Disciples of Christ' and 'Churches of Christ', who now number something like two millions. It comes out of the Presbyterian household. So far as the Ecumenical Movement is concerned, it may be said to be 'born out of due time'. Actually it is a century before its time.

Thomas Campbell, the main author of the document, was born in County Down, Ireland on February 1st, 1763 and died in Bethany, Virginia (now West Virginia) on January 4th, 1854. He was a Minister of what was then known as the Seceder Presbyterian Church in Ahorey, Co. Down, Ireland. For health reasons he emigrated to America in 1807 and became a Minister in West Virginia for the same Church which was there known as the United Presbyterian Church. Dean Frederick D. Kershner of Butler University School of Religion says of him, " He was a man of extraordinary humility and reserve and, while an excellent preacher, was perhaps more famous as a shepherd of the flock." In 1809, because of the scandal of Christian disunity, he decided to withdraw from his allegiance to the Seceder Presbyterian Church and to publish his reasons for so doing in the *Declaration and Address.** It was his first and only important venture into print. By the time it had left the press he had been joined by his family, including his eldest son, Alexander who, educated in the University of Glasgow, had already come to many of the conclusions voiced in the *Declaration and Address* and found himself in full accord with his father. From now on Alexander took the lead in the Reform Movement which the document had set up.

Thomas Campbell had expected his document to produce a religious revolution within a few years. It was a plea for full Christian unity, not on a latitudinarian basis, as the Appendix, written to correct this view, shews; but on the basis of the *facts* of the Gospel as distinct from theological opinions about these facts. The scandal of the disunity of Christians weighed heavily upon his heart and mind. He sought a way to overcome this disunity by a return to the *facts* of the Gospel—the primitive *kerugma*—and a reliance on the New Testament as containing 'all things necessary to salvation'. He recognised the need for theology to safeguard the integrity of the Gospel and to express it in the current thought forms of the day; but he denied that such theological formulation should be made binding upon the sinner seeking salvation and seeking to enter the Church. Salvation depended, rather, upon *personal* faith in and commitment to a personal Lord and Saviour.

He was disappointed in his hopes. Like every great teacher, he was before his time. Only in our day are we seeing the fruits of his hopes and of his work. In his own day the result of his work was, in effect, to set up one

* A first edition of this Document with Appendix is preserved in the Library of Overdale College, Selly Oak, Birmingham.

more Church amongst the many; but that Church, whether in America or the British Isles, has never forgotten that it was born of the passion for Christian unity and that it exists, not as a separate Denomination, but as a Movement within all the Churches to foster the spirit of unity until we all come to "grow up into all things in him, which is the head, even Christ; from whom the whole body fitly framed together, through that which every joint supplieth, according to the working in due measure of each several part, maketh the increase of the body unto the building up of itself in love."* It is for this reason that Disciples (Churches of Christ) have been to the forefront in the modern Ecumenical Movement.†

'Churches of Christ' in this country originated in a similar way from the Movement started by John Glas, Church of Scotland Minister of Teeling, near Dundee, who was deposed in 1730 for objections to State Establishment and to certain tenets of the Westminster Confession of Faith. From the Glasites arose, at the end of the eighteenth century, the Scotch Baptists, a body not to be confused with Baptists in Scotland. William Jones, M.A., who was Minister of the Scotch Baptist Church in London, was from 1830 onwards influenced by the writings of Alexander Campbell and in 1835 and 1836 published a monthly magazine mainly to disseminate Campbell's views. This journal was continued as *The Christian Messenger* (1837–45) by James Wallis of Nottingham, who had been reared in the Scotch Baptist Church in that city. So were gathered together a number of Churches in this country which, in the early years of the nineteenth century, had arisen in various ways, but mostly out of the Scotch Baptist Churches, and which expressed similar ideas to those advocated by the Campbells, pleading for Christian unity on the basis of New Testament faith and practice.‡ The first Annual Conference was held in 1842 at Edinburgh and the second not till 1847 at Chester when Alexander Campbell, who was visiting this country, was President. Close connection with Disciples in America was maintained during the nineteenth century and in 1930 the first World Convention of Churches of Christ was held in Washington, D.C. The second was held in Leicester in 1935 and the third in Buffalo, U.S.A. in 1947. The fourth is planned for 1952 in Melbourne, Australia, where the Movement spread from this country as it did to New Zealand, Canada and South Africa. The American, British, Australian and New Zealand Churches maintain Mission Stations in most parts of the world.

WILLIAM ROBINSON
M.A., B.SC., D.D., S.T.D.
Professor of Christian Doctrine and Theology
The School of Religion, Butler University
Indianapolis, U.S.A.

* Eph. iv, 15, 16.

† It was a Disciple, Dr. Peter Ainslie, who early in this century started *The Christian Union Quarterly*, the precursor of *Christendom*, edited by Dr. Charles Clayton Morrison, another Disciple. This journal eventually became *The Ecumenical Review*, the organ of the World Council of Churches. Disciples have founded two Lectureships on Christian Union, the Hoover Lecture at the University of Chicago and the Peter Ainslie Lecture at Rhodes University, South Africa.

‡ See *What Churches of Christ Stand For*, *The Shattered Cross*, *Discipleship in the Church*, and *Training for Church Membership*, The Berean Press, 20 Brighton Road, Balsall Heath, Birmingham, 12.

DECLARATION AND ADDRESS

Thomas Campbell

1809

THE CHRISTIAN ASSOCIATION OF WASHINGTON, PA., U.S.A.

AT a meeting held at Buffalo, August 17, 1809, consisting of persons of different religious denominations; most of them in an unsettled state as to a fixed gospel ministry; it was unanimously agreed, upon the considerations, and for the purposes herein after declared, to form themselves into a religious association, designated as above—which they accordingly did, and appointed twenty-one of their number to meet and confer together; and, with the assistance of Mr. Thomas Campbell, minister of the gospel, to determine upon the proper means to carry into effect the important ends of their association: the result of which conference was the following declaration and address, agreed upon and ordered to be printed at the expense and for the benefit of the society, September 7, 1809.

DECLARATION, &c.

FROM the series of events which have taken place in the churches for many years past, especially in this western country, as well as from what we know in general of the present state of things in the Christian world, we are persuaded that it is high time for us not only to think, but also to act, for ourselves; to see with our own eyes, and to take all our measures directly and immediately from the Divine Standard. To this alone we feel ourselves divinely bound to be conformed, as by this alone we must be judged. We are also persuaded that, as no man can be *judged* for his brother, so no man can *judge* for his brother; but that every man must be allowed to judge for himself, as every man must bear his own judgment, must give an account of himself to God. We are also of opinion that, as the divine word is equally binding upon all, so all lie under an equal obligation to be bound by it, and it alone; and not by any human interpretation of it: and that, therefore, no man has a right to judge his brother, except in so far as he manifestly violates the express letter of the law; also that every such judgment is an express violation of the law of Christ, a daring usurpation of His throne, and a gross intrusion upon the rights and liberties of His subjects. We are therefore of opinion that we should beware of such things; that we should keep at the utmost distance from every thing of this nature; and that, knowing the judgment of God against them that commit such things, we should neither do the same ourselves, nor have pleasure in them that do them. Moreover, being well aware from sad experience of the heinous nature, and pernicious tendency of religious controversy among Christians, tired and sick of the bitter jarrings and janglings of a party spirit, we would desire to be at rest; and, were it possible, we would also desire to adopt and recommend such measures as would give rest to our brethren throughout all the churches as would restore unity, peace, and purity, to the whole Church of God. This desirable rest, however, we utterly despair either to find for ourselves, or to be able to recommend to our brethren, by continuing amidst the diversity and rancour of party contentions, the veering uncertainty and clashings of human opinions: nor indeed, can we reasonably expect to find it anywhere, but in Christ and His simple word which is the same yesterday, and today, and forever. Our desire, therefore, for ourselves and our brethren would be, that, rejecting human opinions and the inventions of men as of any authority, or as having any place in the Church of God, we might forever cease from farther contentions about such things; returning to, and holding fast by, the original standard; taking the divine word alone for our rule; the Holy Spirit for our teacher and guide, to lead us into all truth; and Christ alone, as exhibited in the word, for our salvation, that, by so doing, we may be at peace among ourselves, follow peace with all men, and holiness, without which no man shall see the Lord. Impressed with these sentiments, we have resolved as follows:

I. That we form ourselves into a religious association under the denomination of the Christian Association of Washington for the sole purpose of promoting simple, evangelical Christianity, free from all mixture of human opinions and inventions of men.

II. That each member, according to ability, cheerfully and liberally subscribe a certain specified sum, to be paid half yearly, for the purpose of raising a fund to support a pure Gospel Ministry that shall reduce to practice that whole form of doctrine, worship, discipline, and government, expressly revealed and enjoined in the word of God; and also for supplying the poor with the Holy Scriptures.

III. That this society consider it a duty, and shall use all proper means in its power, to encourage the formation of similar associations and shall for this purpose hold itself in readiness, upon application, to correspond with, and render all possible assistance to, such as may desire to associate for the same desirable and important purposes.

IV. That this society by no means considers itself a church, nor does at all assume to itself the powers peculiar to such a society: nor do the members, as such, consider themselves as standing connected in that relation; nor as at all associated for the peculiar purposes of church association, but merely as voluntary advocates for church reformation; and, as possessing the powers common to all individuals who may please to associate, in a peaceable and orderly manner, for any lawful purpose: namely, the disposal of their time, counsel and property, as they may see cause.

V. That this society, formed for the sole purpose of promoting simple, evangelical Christianity, shall, to the utmost of its power, countenance and support such ministers, and such only, as exhibit a manifest conformity to the original standard in conversation and doctrine, in zeal and diligence; only such as reduce to practice that simple, original form of Christianity expressly exhibited upon the sacred page; without attempting to inculcate anything of human authority, of private opinion, or inventions of men, as having any place in the constitution, faith, or worship of the Christian Church or anything as matter of Christian faith, or duty, for which there cannot be expressly produced a "thus saith the Lord", either in express terms, or by approved precedent.

VI. That a standing committee of twenty-one members of unexceptionable moral character, inclusive of the secretary and treasurer, be chosen annually to superintend the interests and transact the business, of the society; and that said committee be invested with full powers to act and do, in the name and behalf of their constituents, whatever the society had previously determined, for the purpose of carrying into effect the entire object of its institution; and that in case of any emergency, unprovided for in the existing determinations of the society, said committee be empowered to call a *pro re nota* meeting for that purpose.

VII. That this society meet at least twice a year, viz. on the first Thursday of May and of November, and that the collectors appointed to receive the half-yearly quotas of the promised subscriptions, be in readiness, at or before each meeting, to make their returns to the treasurer, that he may be able to report upon the state of the funds. The next meeting to be held at Washington on the first Thursday of November next.

VIII. That each meeting of the society be opened with a sermon, the constitution and address read, and a collection lifted for the benefit of the society, and that all communications of a public nature be laid before the society at its half-yearly meetings.

IX. That this society, relying upon the all-sufficiency of the Church's Head, and, through His grace, looking with an eye of confidence to the generous liberality of the sincere friends of genuine Christianity, holds itself engaged to afford a competent support to such ministers as the Lord may graciously dispose to assist, at the request and by invitation of the society, in promoting a pure, evangelical reformation, by the simple preaching of the everlasting gospel, and the administration of its ordinances in an exact conformity to the Divine Standard as aforesaid and that, therefore, whatever the friends of the institution shall please to contribute toward the support of ministers in connexion with this society who may be sent forth to preach at considerable distances, the same shall be gratefully received and acknowledged as a donation to its funds.

ADDRESS, &c.

To all that love our Lord Jesus Christ in sincerity, throughout all the Churches, the following Address is most respectfully submitted.

DEARLY BELOVED BRETHREN,

THAT it is the grand design and native tendency of our holy religion to reconcile and unite man to God and to each other, in truth and love, to the glory of God and their own present and eternal good, will not, we presume, be denied by any of the genuine subjects of Christianity. The nativity of its Divine Author was announced from heaven by a host of angels, with high acclamations of "glory to God in the highest, and on earth, peace and good will toward men." The whole tenor of that divine book which contains its institutes, in all its gracious declarations, precepts, ordinances and holy examples, most expressly and powerfully inculcates this. In so far, then, as this holy unity and unanimity in faith and love is attained, just in the same degree, is the glory of God and the happiness of man promoted and secured. Impressed with those sentiments, and at the same time grievously affected with those sad divisions which have so awfully interfered with the benign and gracious intention of our holy religion by exciting its professed subjects to bite and devour one another, we cannot suppose ourselves justifiable in withholding the mite of our sincere and humble endeavours to heal and remove them.

What awful and distressing effects have those sad divisions produced! what adversions, what reproaches, what backbitings, what evil surmisings, what angry contentions, what enmities, what excommunications, and even persecutions! And indeed, this must in some measure continue to be the case so long as those schisms exist, for, said the Apostle, where envying and strife is, *there* is confusion and every evil work. What dreary effects of these accursed divisions are to be seen, even in this highly favoured country, where the sword of the civil magistrate has not, as yet, learned to serve at the altar. Have we not seen congregations broken to pieces, neighbourhoods of professing Christians first thrown into confusion by party contentions and, in the end, entirely deprived of gospel ordinances; while in the meantime, large settlements and tracts of country remain to this day entirely destitute of a gospel ministry; many of them in little better than a state of heathenism, the churches being either so weakened with divisions that they cannot send them ministers or, the people so divided among themselves that they will not receive them? Several at the same time who live at the door of a preached gospel, dare not in conscience go to hear it, and, of course, enjoy little more advantage in that respect, than if living in the midst of heathens. How seldom do many in those circumstances enjoy the dispensation of the Lord's Supper, that great ordinance of unity and love! How sadly, also, does this broken and confused state of things interfere with that spiritual intercourse amongst Christians, one with another, which is so essential to their edification and comfort in the midst of a present evil world, so divided in sentiment, and, of course, living at such distances, that but few of the same opinion or party, can conveniently and frequently assemble for religious purposes, or enjoy a due frequency of ministerial attentions. And even where things are in a better state with respect to settled churches, how is the tone of discipline relaxed under the influence of a party spirit, many being afraid to exercise it with due strictness, lest their people should leave them and, under the cloak of some specious pretence, find refuge in the bosom of another party; while, lamentable to be told, so corrupt is the Church with those accursed divisions, that there are but few so base as not to find admission into some professing party or other. Thus, in a great measure, is that scriptural purity of communion banished from the Church of God, upon the due preservation of which, much of her comfort, glory, and usefulness depend. To complete the dread result of our woeful divisions, one evil yet remains of a very awful nature: the divine displeasure justly provoked with this sad perversion of the gospel of peace, the Lord withholds His gracious influential presence from His ordinances and, not unfrequently, gives up the contentious authors and abettors of religious discord to fall into grievous scandals, or visits them with judgments, as he did the house of Eli. Thus, while professing Christians bite and devour one another, they are consumed one of another, or fall a prey to the righteous judgment of God. Meantime the truly religious of all parties are grieved, the weak stumbled, the graceless and profane hardened, the mouths of infidels opened to blaspheme religion; and thus the only thing under heaven, divinely efficacious to promote and secure the present spiritual and eternal good of man, even the gospel of the blessed Jesus, is reduced to contempt; while multitudes deprived of the gospel ministry, as has been observed, fall an easy pray to seducers and so become the dupes of almost unheard of delusions. Are not such the visible effects of our sad divisions even in this otherwise happy country? Say, dear brethren, are not these things so? Is it not then your incumbent duty to endeavour, by all scriptural means, to have those evils remedied? Who will say, that it is not? And does it not peculiarly belong to *you*, who occupy the place of gospel ministers, to be leaders in this laudable undertaking? Much depends upon *your* hearty concurrence and zealous endeavours. The favourable opportunity which Divine Providence has put into your hands, in this happy country, for the accomplishment of so great a good is, in itself, a consideration of no small encouragement. A country happily exempted from the baneful influence of a civil establishment of any peculiar form of Christianity, from under the direct influence of the anti-Christian hierarchy, and, at the same time, from any formal connexion with the devoted nations that have given their strength and power unto the beast; in which, of course, no adequate reformation can be accomplished, until the word of God is fulfilled, and the vials of His wrath poured out upon them. Happy exemption, indeed, from being the object of such awful judgments. Still more happy will it be for us, if we duly esteem and improve those great advantages, for the high and valuable ends for which they are manifestly given; and sure where much is given, much also will be required. Can the Lord expect, or require, anything less, from a people in such unhampered circumstances, from a people so liberally furnished with all means and mercies, than a thorough reformation in all things civil and religious, according to his word? Why should we suppose it? And would not such an improvement of our precious privileges be equally conducive to the glory of God and our own present and everlasting good? The auspicious phenomena of the times furnish collateral arguments of a very encouraging nature, that our dutiful and pious endeavours shall not be in vain in the Lord. Is it not the day of the Lord's vengeance upon the anti-Christian world; the year of recompences for the controversy of Zion? Surely then the time to favour her is come; even the set time. And is it not said that Zion shall be built in troublous times? Have not greater efforts been made, and more done, for the promulgation of the gospel among the nations, since the commencement of the French revolution than had been for many centuries prior to that event? And have not the churches both in Europe and America, since that period discovered a more than usual concern for the removal of contentions, for the healing of divisions, for the restoration of a Christian and brotherly intercourse one with another, and for the promotion of each other's spiritual good; as the printed documents, upon those subjects, amply testify? Should *we* not, then, be excited by these considerations to concur with all our might, to help forward this good work, that what yet remains to be done may be fully accomplished? And what! Though the well meant endeavours after union have not, in some instances, entirely succeeded to this wish of all parties, should this dissuade us from the attempt? Indeed, should Christians cease to contend earnestly for the sacred articles of faith and duty once delivered to the saints, on account of the opposition and scanty success which, in many instances attend their faithful and honest endeavours, the divine cause of truth and righteousness might have, long ago, been relinquished. And is there any thing more formidable in the Goliath-schism, than in many other evils which Christians have to combat? Or, has the Captain of Salvation sounded a desist from pursuing, or proclaimed a truce with, this deadly enemy that is sheathing its sword in the very bowels of His Church, rending and mangling His mystical body into pieces? Has He said to His servants let it alone? If not, where is the warrant for a cessation of endeavours to have it removed? On the other hand, are we not the better instructed by sage experience, how to proceed in this business, having before our eyes the inadvertencies and mistakes of others, which have hitherto, in many instances, prevented the desired success? Thus, taught by experience, and happily furnished with the accumulated instructions of those that have gone before us, earnestly labouring in this good cause, let us take unto ourselves the whole armour of God, and, having our feet shod with the preparation of the gospel of peace, let us stand fast by this important duty, with all perseverance. Let none that love the peace of Zion be discouraged, much less offended, because that an object of such magnitude does not, in the first instance, come forth recommended by the express suffrage of the mighty or the many. This consideration, if duly weighed, will neither give offence, nor yield discouragement, to any, that considers the nature of the thing in question, in connexion with what has been already suggested. Is it not a matter of universal right, a duty equally belonging to every citizen of Zion, to seek her good? In this respect, no one can claim a preference above his fellows, as to any peculiar, much less exclusive, obligation. And, as for authority, it can have no place in this business; for surely none can suppose themselves invested with a divine right, as to any thing peculiarly belonging to them, to call the attention of their brethren to this dutiful and important undertaking. For our part, we entertain no such arrogant presumption; nor are we inclined to impute the thought to any of our brethren, that this work should be let alone till such time as they may think proper to come forward, and sanction the attempt by their invitation and example. It is an open field, an extensive work, to which all are equally welcome, equally invited.

Should we speak of competency, viewing the greatness of the object and the manifold difficulties which lie in the way of its accomplishment, we would readily exclaim, with the Apostle, Who is sufficient for these things! But, upon recollecting ourselves, neither would *we* be discouraged, persuaded with him, that, as the work in which we are engaged, so likewise *our* sufficiency, is of God. But, after all, both the mighty and the many are with us. The Lord himself, and all that are truly His people, are declaredly on our side. The prayers of all the churches, nay, the prayers of Christ Himself, (John 17, 20, 23) and of all that have ascended to His heavenly kingdom, are with us. The blessing out of Zion is pronounced upon our undertaking. "Pray for the peace of Jerusalem, they shall prosper that love thee." With such encouragements as these, what should deter us from the heavenly enterprise, or render hopeless the attempt of accomplishing, in due time, an entire union of all the churches in faith and practice, according to the word of God? Not that we judge ourselves competent to effect such a thing; we utterly disclaim the thought: but we judge it our bounden duty to make the attempt, by using all due means in our power to promote it; and also that we have sufficient reason to rest assured that our humble and well-meant endeavours shall not be in vain in the Lord.

The cause that we advocate is not our own peculiar, nor the cause of any party, considered as such; it is a common cause, the cause of Christ and our brethren of all denominations. All that we presume, then, is to do what we humbly conceive to be *our* duty, in connexion with our brethren, to all of whom it equally belongs, as to us, to exert themselves for this blessed purpose. And as we have no just reason to doubt the concurrence of our brethren to accomplish an object so desirable in itself and fraught with such happy consequences, so neither can we look forward to that happy event, which will forever put an end to our hapless divisions, and restore to the Church its primitive unity, purity and prosperity, but in the pleasing prospect of their hearty and dutiful concurrence.

Dearly beloved brethen, why should *we* deem it a thing incredible that the Church of Christ in this highly favoured country should resume that original unity, peace and purity, which belongs to its constitution, and constitutes its glory? Or, is there any thing that can be justly deemed necessary for this desirable purpose, but to conform to the model and adopt the practice of the primitive Church, expressly exhibited in the New Testament? Whatever alterations this might produce in any or all of the churches, should, we think, neither be deemed inadmissible nor ineligible. Surely such alteration would be every way for the better and not for the worse; unless we should suppose the divinely inspired rule to be faulty, or defective. Were we, then, in our Church constitution and managements, to exhibit a complete conformity to the Apostolic Church, would we not be in that respect, as perfect as Christ intended we should be? And should not this suffice us?

It is, to us, a pleasing consideration that all the churches of Christ, which mutually acknowledge each other as such, are not only agreed in the great doctrines of faith and holiness, but are also materially agreed, as to the positive ordinances of Gospel institution; so that our differences, at most, are about the things in which the kingdom of God does not consist, that is, about matters of private opinion, or human invention. What a pity, that the kingdom of God should be divided about such things! Who, then, would not be the first amongst us to give up with human inventions in the worship of God, and to cease from imposing his private opinions upon his brethen, that our breaches might *thus* be healed? Who would not willingly conform to the original pattern laid down in the New Testament, for *this* happy purpose? Our dear brethren, of all denominations, will please to consider, that we have our educational prejudices and particular customs to struggle with as well as they. But this we do sincerely declare, that there is nothing we have hitherto received as matter of faith or practice which is not expressly taught and enjoined in the word of God, either in express terms, or approved precedent, that we would not heartily relinquish, that so we might return to the original constitutional unity of the Christian Church, and, in this happy unity, enjoy full communion with all our brethren, in peace and charity. The like dutiful condescension we candidly expect of all that are seriously impressed with a sense of the duty they owe to God, to each other and to their perishing fellow-brethren of mankind. To this we call, we invite, our brethren of all denominations, by all the sacred motives which we have avouched as the impulsive reasons of our thus addressing them.

You are all, dear brethren, equally included as the object of our love and esteem. With you all we desire to unite in the bonds of an entire Christian unity, Christ alone being the head, the centre; his word the rule; an explicit belief of, and manifest comformity to it in all things, *the terms*. More than this, you will not require of us; and less we cannot require of you; nor indeed, can we reasonably suppose, any would desire it; for what good purpose would it serve? We dare neither assume, nor purpose, the trite indefinite distinction between essentials and non-essentials in matters of revealed truth and duty; firmly persuaded, that, whatever may be their comparative importance, simply considered, the high obligation of the Divine Authority revealing, or enjoining them, renders the belief, or performance of them, absolutely essential to us, in so far as we know them. And to be ignorant of anything God has revealed, can neither be our duty, nor our privilege. We humbly presume then, dear brethren, you can have no relevant objection to meet us upon this ground. And, we again beseech you, let it be known, that it is the invitation but of a few; by your accesions we shall be many; and whether few or many, in the first instance, it is all one with respect to the event, which must ultimately await the full information, and hearty concurrence, of all. Besides, whatever is to be done, must begin, sometime, somewhere; and no matter where, nor by whom, if the Lord puts his hand to the work, it must surely prosper. And has he not been graciously pleased, upon many signal occasions, to bring to pass the greatest events from very small beginnings, and even by means the most unlikely? Duty then is ours; but events belong to God.

We hope, then, what we urge, will neither be deemed an unreasonable nor an unseasonable undertaking. Why should it be thought unseasonable? Can any time be assigned, while things continue as they are, that would prove more favourable for such an attempt, or what could be supposed to make it so? Might it be the approximation of parties to a greater nearness, in point of public profession and similarity of customs? Or, might it be expected from a gradual decline of bigotry? As to the former, it is a well known fact, that where the difference is least, the opposition is always managed with a degree of vehemence, inversely proportioned to the merits of the cause. With respect to the latter, though we are happy to say that, in some cases and places and, we hope, universally, bigotry is upon the decline, yet we are not warranted either by the past or present, to act upon that supposition. We have, as yet, by this means, seen no such effect produced; nor indeed could we reasonably expect it; for there will always be multitudes of weak persons in the church, and these are generally most subject to bigotry; add to this, that, while divisions exist, there will always be found interested men, who will not fail to support them: nor can we at all suppose that Satan will be idle to improve an advantage so important to the interests of his kingdom. And, let it be further observed upon the whole, that, in matters of similar importance to our secular interests, we would by no means content ourselves with such kind of reasoning. We might further add that, the attempt here suggested not being of a partial, but of general nature, it can have no just tendency to excite the jealousy, or hurt the feelings, of any party. On the contrary, every effort towards a permanent scriptural unity amongst the churches upon the solid basis of universally acknowledged, and self-evident truths, must have the happiest tendency to enlighten and conciliate, by thus manifesting to each other their mutual charity, and zeal for the truth: "Whom I loved in the truth," saith the Apostle, "and not I only, but also all they that have known the truth; for the truth's sake, which is in us, and shall be with us forever." Indeed, if no such divine and adequate basis of union can be fairly exhibited as will meet the approbation of every upright and intelligent Christian, nor such mode of procedure adopted in favour of the weak as will not oppress their consciences, then the accomplishment of this grand object upon principle, must be forever impossible. There would, upon this supposition, remain no other way of accomplishing it, but merely by voluntary compromise and good natured accommodation. That such a thing however will be accomplished, one way or other, will not be questioned by any that allow themselves to believe that the commands and prayers of our Lord Jesus Christ will not utterly prove ineffectual. Whatever way, then, it is to be effected, whether upon the solid basis of divinely revealed truth, or the good natured principle of Christian forbearance and gracious condescension, is it not equally practicable, equally eligible to us, as ever it can be to any; unless we should suppose ourselves destitute of that Christian temper and discernment, which is essentially necessary to qualify us to do the will of our gracious Redeemer, Whose expressed command to His people is that there be no division among them, but that they all walk by the same rule, speak the same thing, and be perfectly joined together in the same mind, and in the same judgment? We believe, then, it is as practicable as it is eligible. Let us attempt it. "Up and be doing, and the Lord will be with you."

Are we not all praying for that happy event, when there shall be but one fold, as there is but one Chief Shepherd? What! shall we pray for a thing and not strive to obtain it! not use the necessary means to have it accomplished! What said the Lord to Moses upon a piece of conduct somewhat similar? "Why criest thou unto Me? Speak unto the children of Israel that they go forward, but lift thou up thy rod, and stretch out thine hand." Let the ministers of Jesus but embrace this exhortation, put their hand to the work and encourage the people to go forward upon the firm ground of obvious truth, to unite in the bonds of an entire Christian unity, and who will venture to say that it would not soon be accomplished? "Cast ye up, cast ye up, prepare the way, take up the stumbling block out of the way of My people," saith your God. To you, therefore, it peculiarly belongs, as the professed and acknowledged leaders of the people, to go before them in this good work, to remove human opinions and the inventions of men out of the way; by carefully separating this chaff from the pure wheat of primary and authentic revelation; casting out that assumed authority, that enacting and decreeing power, by which those things have been imposed and established. To the ministerial department then do we look with anxiety. Ministers of Jesus, we can neither be ignorant of, nor unaffected with, the divisions and corruptions of His Church. His dying commands, His last and ardent prayers for the visible unity of His professing people, will not suffer you to be indifferent in this matter. You will not, you cannot, therefore, be silent, upon a subject of such vast importance to His personal glory and the happiness of His people, consistently you cannot; for silence gives consent. You will rather lift up your voice like a trumpet to expose the heinous nature and dreadful consequences of those unnatural and anti-Christian divisions which have so rent and ruined the church of God. Thus, in justice to your station and character, honoured of the Lord, would we hopefully anticipate your zealous and faithful efforts to heal the breaches of Zion; that God's dear children might dwell together in unity and love. But if otherwise—* * * * we forebear to utter it. See Mal. 2, 1—10.

Oh! that ministers and people would but consider, that there are no divisions in the grave; nor in that world which lies beyond it: there our divisions must come to an end. We must all unite there. Would to God we could find in our hearts to put an end to our short-lived divisions here, that so we might leave a blessing behind us, even a happy and united church! What gratification, what utility, in the meantime, can our divisions afford either to ministers or people? Should they be perpetuated till the day of judgment, would they convert one sinner from the error of his ways, or save a soul from death? Have they any tendency to hide the multitude of sins that are so dishonourable to God and hurtful to His people? Do they not rather irritate and produce them? How innumerable and highly aggravated are the sins they have produced and are, at this day, producing, both amongst professors and profane. We entreat, we beseech you then, dear brethren, by all those considerations, to concur in this blessed and dutiful attempt. What is the work of all, must be done by all. Such was the work of the tabernacle in the wilderness. Such is the work to which you are called; not by the authority of man, but by Jesus Christ and God the Father, who raised Him from the dead. By this authority are you called to raise up the tabernacle of David, that is fallen down amongst us, and to set it up upon its own base. This you cannot do, while you run every man to his own house, and consult only the interest of his own party. Till you associate, consult, and advise together, and in a friendly and Christian manner explore the subject, nothing can be done. We would therefore, with all due deference and submission, call the attention of our brethren to the obvious and important duty of association. Unite with us in the common cause of simple, evangelical Christianity. In this glorious cause we are ready to unite with you. United we shall prevail. It is the cause of Christ, and of our brethren throughout all the churches, of catholic unity, peace, and purity, a cause that must finally prosper in spite of all opposition. Let us unite to promote it. Come forward then, dear brethren and help with us. Do not suffer yourselves to be lulled asleep by that syren song of the slothful and reluctant professor, "The time is not yet come, the time is not come, saith he, the time that the Lord's house should be built." Believe him not. Do ye not discern the signs of the times? "Have not the two witnesses arisen from their state of political death, from under the long proscription of ages? Have they not stood upon their feet, in the presence and to the consternation and terror of their enemies? Has not their resurrection been accompanied with a great earthquake? Has not the tenth part of the great city been thrown down by it? Has not this event aroused the nations to indignation? Have they not been angry, yea very angry? Therefore, O Lord, is Thy wrath come upon them, and the time of the dead that they should be avenged, and that thou shouldest give reward to thy servants, the Prophets, and to them that fear thy name, both small and great; and that thou shouldest destroy them that have destroyed the earth." Who amongst us has not heard the report of these things, of these lightnings and thunderings, and voices of this tremendous earthquake and great hail; of these awful convulsions and revolutions that have dashed and are dashing to pieces the nations like a potter's vessel? Yea, have not the remote vibrations of this dreadful shock been felt even by us, whom Providence has graciously placed at so great a distance? What shall we say to these things? Is it time for us to sit still in our corruptions and divisions, when the Lord by His word and providence, is so loudly and expressly calling us to repentance and reformation? "Awake, awake; put on thy strength, O Zion, put on thy beautiful garments, O Jerusalem the holy city; for henceforth there shall no more come unto thee the uncircumcised and the unclean. Shake thyself from the dust, O Jerusalem; arise, loose thyself from the *bands* of thy neck, O captive daughter of Zion." Resume that precious, that dear bought liberty, wherewith Christ has made His people free; a liberty from subjection to any authority but His own, in matters of religion. "Call no man father, no man master upon earth; for one is your master, even Christ, and all ye are brethren." Stand fast therefore in this precious liberty, and be not entangled again with the yoke of bondage.

For the vindication of this precious liberty have we declared ourselves hearty and willing advocates. For this benign and dutiful purpose have we associated, that by so doing, we might contribute the mite of our humble endeavours to promote it, and thus invite our brethren to do the same. As the first fruits of our efforts for this blessed purpose we respectfully present to their consideration the following propositions, relying upon their charity and candour that they will neither despise, nor misconstrue, our humble and adventurous attempt. If they should in any measure serve, as a preliminary, to open up the way to a permanent scriptural unity amongst the friends and lovers of truth and peace throughout the churches, we shall greatly rejoice at it. We by no means pretend to dictate: and could we propose any thing more evident, consistent, and adequate, it should be at their service. Their pious and dutiful attention to an object of such magnitude will induce them to communicate to us their emendations; and thus what is sown in weakness, will be raised up in power; for certainly the collective graces that are conferred upon the church, if duly united and brought to bear upon any point of commanded duty, would be amply sufficient for the right and successful performance of it. "For to one is given by the spirit the word of wisdom; to another the word of knowledge by the same spirit; to another faith by the same spirit; to another the discerning of spirits: but the manifestation of the spirit is given to every man to profit withal. As every man, therefore, hath received the gift, even so minister the same one to another as good stewards of the manifold grace of God." In the face then of such instructions, and with such assurances of an all-sufficiency of divine grace, as the Church has received from her exalted Head, we can neither justly doubt the concurrence of her genuine members, nor yet their ability, when dutifully acting together, to accomplish any thing that is necessary for His glory and their own good; and certainly their visible unity in truth and holiness, in faith and love, is, of all things, the most conducive to both these, if we may credit the dying commands and prayers of our gracious Lord. In a matter, therefore, of such confessed importance, our Christian brethren, however unhappily distinguished by party names, will not, cannot, withhold their helping hand. We are as heartily willing to be their debtors, as they are indispensably bound to be our benefactors. Come, then, dear brethren, we most humbly beseech you, cause your light to shine upon our weak beginnings, that we may see to work by it. Evince your zeal for the glory of Christ, and the spiritual welfare of your fellow-Christians, by your hearty and zealous co-operation to promote the unity, purity and prosperity of His church.

Let none imagine that the subjoined propositions are at all intended as an overture towards a new creed, or standard, for the church, or, as in any wise designed to be made a term of communion; nothing can be farther from our intention. They are merely designed for opening up the way, that we may come fairly and firmly to original ground upon clear and certain premises, and take up things just as the Apostles left them, that, thus disentangled from the accruing embarrassments of intervening ages, we may stand with evidence upon the same ground on which the Church stood at the beginning. Having said so much to solicit attention and prevent mistake, we submit as follows:

PROP. 1. THAT the Church of Christ upon earth is essentially, intentionally, and constitutionally one, consisting of all those in every place that profess their faith in Christ and obedience to Him in all things according to the scriptures, and that manifest the same by their tempers and conduct, and of none else, as none else can be truly and properly called Christians.

2. That although the Church of Christ upon earth must necessarily exist in particular and distinct societies, locally separate one from another, yet there ought to be no schisms, no uncharitable divisions among them. They ought to receive each other as Christ Jesus hath also received them to the glory of God. And for this purpose, they ought all to walk by the same rule, to mind and speak the same thing and to be perfectly joined together in the same mind and the same judgment.

3. That in order to this, nothing ought to be inculcated upon Christians as articles of faith, nor required of them as terms of communion, but what is expressly taught and enjoined upon them in the word of God. Nor ought anything be admitted as of divine obligation in their church constitution and managements, but what is expressly enjoined by the authority of our Lord Jesus Christ and His Apostles upon the New Testament Church, either in expressed terms, or by approved precedent.

4. That although the scriptures of the Old and New Testament are inseparably connected, making together but one perfect and entire revelation of the Divine will, for the edification and salvation of the Church, and therefore in that respect cannot be separated, yet as to what directly and properly belongs to their immediate object, the New Testament is as perfect a constitution for the worship, discipline and government of the New Testament Church, and as perfect a rule for the particular duties of its members, as the Old Testament was for the worship, discipline and government of the Old Testament Church, and the particular duties of its members.

5. That with respect to the commands and ordinances of our Lord Jesus Christ, where the scriptures are silent, as to the express time or manner of performance, if any such there be, no human authority has power to interfere, in order to supply the supposed deficiency, by making laws for the Church; nor can any thing more be required of Christians in such cases, but only that they *so* observe these commands and ordinances, as will evidently answer the declared and obvious end of their institution. Much less has any human authority power to impose new commands or ordinances upon the Church, which our Lord Jesus Christ has not enjoined. Nothing ought to be received into the faith or worship of the Church, or be made a term of communion amongst Christians, that is not as old as the New Testament.

6. That although inferences and deductions from scripture premises, when fairly inferred, may be truly called the doctrine of God's holy word, yet are they not formally binding upon the consciences of Christians farther than they perceive the connexion, and evidently see that they are so; for their faith must not stand in the wisdom of men, but in the power and veracity of God. Therefore no such deduction can be made terms of communion, but do properly belong to the after and progressive edification of the Church. Hence it is evident that no such deductions or inferential truths ought to have any place in the Church's confession.

7. That although doctrinal exhibitions of the great system of divine truths and defensive testimonies in opposition to prevailing errors, be highly expedient, and the more full and explicit they be for those purposes, the better, yet as these must be in a great measure the effect of human reasoning, and of course must contain many inferential truths, they ought not to be made terms of Christian communion; unless we suppose, what is contrary to fact, that none have a right to the communion of the Church but such as possess a very clear and decisive judgment, or are come to a very high degree of doctrinal information; whereas the Church from the beginning did, and ever will, consist of little children and young men as well as fathers.

8. That as it is not necessary that persons should have a particular knowledge or distinct apprehension of all divinely revealed truths in order to entitle them to a place in the Church, neither should they, for this purpose, be required to make a profession more extensive than their knowledge; but that, on the contrary, their having a due measure of scriptural self-knowledge respecting their lost and perishing condition by nature and practice, and of the way of salvation through Jesus Christ, accompanied with a profession of their faith in, and obedience to Him in all things according to His word, is all that is absolutely necessary to qualify them for admission into His Church.

9. That all that are enabled, through grace, to make such a profession, and to manifest the reality of it in their tempers and conduct, should consider each other as the precious saints of God, should love each other as brethren, children of the same family and Father, temples of the same Spirit, members of the same Body, subjects of the same grace, objects of the same divine love, bought with the same price, and joint heirs of the same inheritance. Whom God hath thus joined together no man should dare to put asunder.

10. That division among Christians is a horrid evil, fraught with many evils. It is anti-Christian, as it destroys the visible unity of the Body of Christ; as if He were divided against Himself, excluding and excommunicating a part of Himself. It is anti-scriptural, as being strictly prohibited by His sovereign authority; a direct violation of His express command. It is anti-natural, as it excites Christians to condemn, to hate and oppose one another, who are bound by the highest and most endearing obligations to love each other as brethren, even as Christ has loved them. In a word, it is productive of confusion and of every evil work.

11. That, in some instances, a partial neglect of the expressly revealed will of God and, in others, an assumed authority for making the approbation of human opinions and human inventions a term of communion by introducing them into the constitution, faith, or worship, of the Church are, and have been, the immediate, obvious and universally acknowledged causes of all the corruptions and divisions that ever have taken place in the Church of God.

12. That all that is necessary to the highest state of perfection and purity of the Church upon earth is, first, that none be received as members but such as, having that due measure of scriptural self-knowledge described above, do profess their faith in Christ and obedience to Him in all things according to the scriptures; nor, secondly, that any be retained in her communion longer than they continue to manifest the reality of their profession by their tempers and conduct. Thirdly, that her ministers, duly and scripturally qualified,

inculcate none other things than those very articles of faith and holiness expressly revealed and enjoined in the word of God. Lastly, that in all their administration they keep close by the observance of all divine ordinances, after the example of the primitive Church, exhibited in the New Testament, without any additions whatsoever of human opinions or inventions of men.

13. Lastly. That if any circumstantial, indispensably necessary to the observance of divine ordinances, be not found upon the page of express revelation, such, and such only, as are absolutely necessary for this purpose should be adopted, under the title of human expedients, without any pretence to a more sacred origin; so that any subsequent alteration or difference in the observance of these things might produce no contention nor division in the Church.

From the nature and construction of these propositions it will evidently appear, that they are laid in a designed subserviency to the declared end of our association, and are exhibited for the express purpose of performing a duty of previous necessity; a duty loudly called for in existing circumstances at the hands of every one that would desire to promote the interests of Zion; a duty not only enjoined, as has been already observed from Is. 57, 14, but which is also there predicted of the faithful remnant as a thing in which they would voluntarily engage. "He that putteth his trust in Me shall possess the land, and shall inherit My holy mountain; and shall say, cast ye up, cast ye up, prepare the way; take up the stumbling block out of the way of My people."

To prepare the way for a permanent scriptural unity amongst Christians, by calling up to their consideration fundamental truths, directing their attention to first principles, clearing the way before them by removing the stumbling blocks, the rubbish of ages which has been thrown upon it and fencing it on each side, that in advancing towards the desired object, they may not miss the way through mistake, or inadvertency, by turning aside to the right hand or to the left, is, at least, the sincere intention of the above propositions. It remains with our brethren now to say how far they go toward answering this intention. Do they exhibit truths demonstrably evident in the light of scripture and right reason, so that, to deny any part of them, the contrary assertion would be manifestly absurd and inadmissible? Considered as a preliminary for the above purpose, are they adequate; so that if acted upon, they would infallibly lead to the desired issue? If evidently defective in either of these respects, let them be corrected and amended, till they become sufficiently evident, adequate, and unexceptionable. In the meantime let them be examined with rigour, with all the rigour that justice, candour, and charity will admit. If we have mistaken the way, we shall be glad to be set right; but if, in the mean time, we have been happily led to suggest obvious and undeniable truths, which, if adopted and acted upon, would infallibly lead to the desired unity, and secure it when obtained, we hope it will be no objection, that they have not proceeded from a general council. It is not the voice of the multitude, but the voice of truth, that has power with the conscience, that can produce rational conviction and acceptable obedience. A conscience that awaits the decision of the multitude, that hangs in suspense for the casting vote of the majority, is a fit subject for the man of sin. This we are persuaded is the uniform sentiment of real Christians of every denomination. Would to God that all professors were such. Then should our eyes soon behold the prosperity of Zion. We should soon see Jerusalem a quiet habitation. Union in truth has been, and ever must be, the desire and prayer of all such. Union in Truth is our motto. The Divine Word is our Standard. In the Lord's name do we display our banners. Our eyes are upon the promises, "So shall they fear the name of the Lord from the west, and his glory from the rising of the sun." "When the enemy shall come in like a flood the spirit of the Lord shall lift up a standard against him." Our humble desire is to be His standard bearers to fight under *His* banner, and with *His* weapons, "which are not carnal, but mighty through God to the pulling down of strong holds;" even all these strong holds of division, those partition walls of separation, which, like the wall of Jericho, have been built up, as it were, to the very heavens, to separate God's people, to divide *His* flock and so to prevent them from entering into their promised rest, at least in so far as it respects this world. An enemy hath done this; but he shall not finally prevail; for "the meek shall inherit the earth and shall delight themselves in the abundance of peace." "And the kingdom and dominion, even the greatness of the kingdom under the whole heaven, shall be given to the people of the saints of the Most High, and they shall possess it forever." But this cannot be in their present broken and divided state, "for a kingdom, or an house, divided against itself cannot stand, but cometh to desolation." Now this has been the case with the Church for a long time. However, "the Lord will not cast off his people, neither will he forsake his heritage, but judgment shall return unto righteousness, and all the upright in heart shall follow it." To all such, and such alone, are our expectations directed. Come, then, ye blessed of the Lord, we have your prayers; let us also have your actual assistance. What, shall we pray for a thing and not strive to obtain it!

We call, we invite you again, by every consideration in these premises. You that are near, associate with us; you that are at too great a distance, associate as we have done. Let not the paucity of your number in any given district prove an insuperable discouragement. Remember Him that has said, "if two of you shall agree on earth as touching anything that they shall ask, it shall be done for them of My Father which is in heaven: for where two or three are gathered together in My name, there am I in the midst of them." With such a promise as this for the attainment of every possible and promised good, there is no room for discouragement. Come on, then, "ye that fear the Lord keep not silence, and give him no rest till he make Jerusalem a joy and a praise in the earth." Put on that noble resolution dictated by the prophet, saying, "for Zion's sake will we not hold our peace, and for Jerusalem's sake we will not rest, until the righteousness thereof go forth as brightness, and the salvation thereof as a lamp that burneth." Thus impressed, ye will find means to associate at such convenient distances as to meet, at least, once a month, to beseech the Lord to put an end to our lamentable divisions, to heal and unite His people, that His church may resume her original constitutional unity and purity and thus be exalted to the enjoyment of her promised prosperity, that the Jews may be speedily converted, and the fullness of the Gentiles brought in. Thus associated, you will be in a capacity to investigate the evil causes of our sad divisions, to consider and bewail their pernicious effects, and to mourn over them before the Lord, Who hath said, "I will go and return to my place, till they acknowledge their offence and seek my face." Alas! then, what reasonable prospect can we have of being delivered from those sad calamities which have so long afflicted the Church of God, while a party spirit, instead of bewailing, is everywhere justifying the bitter principle of these pernicious evils; by insisting upon the right of rejecting those, however unexceptionable in other respects, who cannot see with them in matters of private opinion, of human inference, that are nowhere expressly revealed or enjoined in the word of God? Thus associated, will the friends of peace, the advocates for Christian unity, be in a capacity to connect in large circles, where several of those smaller societies may meet semi-annually at a convenient centre, and thus avail themselves of their combined exertions for promoting the interests of the common cause. We hope that many of the Lord's ministers in all places will volunteer in this service, forasmuch as they know, it is His favourite work, the very desire of His soul.

Ye lovers of Jesus, and beloved of Him, however scattered in this cloudy and dark day, ye love the truth as it is in Jesus, if our hearts deceive us not; so do we. Ye desire union in Christ, with all them that love Him; so do we. Ye lament and bewail our sad divisions; so do we. Ye reject the doctrines and commandments of men that ye may keep the law of Christ; so do we. Ye believe the alone sufficiency of His word; so do we. Ye believe that the word itself ought to be our rule and not any human explication of it; so do we. Ye believe that no man has a right to judge, to exclude or reject, his professing Christian brother, except in so far as he stands condemned, or rejected, by the express letter of the law; so do we. Ye believe that the great fundamental law of unity and love ought not to be violated to make way for exalting human opinions to an equality with express revelation, by making them articles of faith and terms of communion; so do we. Ye sincere and impartial followers of Jesus, friends of truth and peace, we dare not, we cannot, think otherwise of you; it would be doing violence to your character; it would be inconsistent with your prayers and profession so to do. We shall therefore have *your* hearty concurrence. But if any of our dear brethren, from whom we should expect better things, should through weakness or prejudice be in any thing otherwise minded than we have ventured to suppose, we charitably hope that, in due time, God will reveal even this unto them. Only let such neither refuse to come to the light nor yet through prejudice, reject it, when it shines upon them. Let them rather seriously consider what we have thus most seriously and respectfully submitted to their consideration, weigh every sentiment in the balance of the sanctuary, as in the sight of God, with earnest prayer for and humble reliance upon His Spirit, and not in the spirit of self-sufficiency and party zeal; and in so doing, we rest assured, the consequence will be happy, both for their own, and the Church's peace. Let none imagine that, in so saying, we arrogate to ourselves a degree of intelligence superior to our brethren, much less superior to mistake; so far from this, our confidence is entirely founded upon the express scripture and matter of fact evidence of the things referred to; which may nevertheless, through inattention, or prejudice, fail to produce their proper effect; as has been the case with respect to some of the most evident truths in a thousand instances. But "charity thinketh no evil" and we are far from surmising, though we must speak. To warn even against possible evils is certainly no breach of charity, as to be confident of the certainty of some things is no just argument of presumption. We by no means claim the approbation of our brethren as to any thing we have suggested for promoting the sacred cause of Christian unity, farther than it carries its own evidence along with it; but we humbly claim a fair investigation of the subject and solicit the assistance of our brethren for carrying into effect what we have thus weakly attempted. It is our consolation, in the mean time, that the desired event, as certain as it will be happy and glorious, admits of no dispute, however we may hesitate, or differ, about the proper means of promoting it. All we shall venture to say as to this, is that we trust we have taken the proper ground, at least; if we have not, we despair of finding it elsewhere. For if, holding fast in profession and practice whatever is expressly revealed and enjoined in the divine standard, does not, under the promised influence of the divine Spirit, prove an adequate basis for promoting and maintaining unity, peace and purity, we utterly despair of attaining those invaluable privileges by adopting the standard of any party. To advocate the cause of unity while espousing the interests of a party would appear as absurd, as for this country to take part with either of the belligerents in the present awful struggle, which has convulsed and is convulsing the nations, in order to maintain her neutrality and secure her peace. Nay, it would be adopting the very means by which the bewildered Church has, for hundreds of years past, been rending and dividing herself into fractions; for Christ's sake and for the truth's sake; though the first and foundation truth of our Christianity is union with Him, and the very next to it in order, union with each other in Him; "that we receive each other, as Christ has also received us, to the glory of God." "For this is His commandment that we believe in His Son Jesus Christ, and love one another, as He gave us commandment. And he that keepeth His commandments dwelleth in Him, and He in him; and hereby we know that He dwelleth in us, by the spirit which He hath given us", even the spirit of faith, and of love, and of a sound mind. And surely this should suffice us. But how to love and receive our brother, as we believe and hope Christ has received both him and us, and yet refuse to hold communion with him is, we confess, a mystery too deep for us. If this be the way that Christ hath received us, then woe is unto us. We do not here intend a professed brother trangressing the expressed letter of the law, and refusing to be reclaimed. Whatever may be our charity in such a case, we have not sufficient evidence that Christ hath received him, or that he hath received Christ as his teacher and Lord. To adopt means, then, apparently subversive of the very end proposed, means which the experience of ages has evinced successful only in overthrowing the visible interests of Christianity, in counteracting, as far as possible, the declared intention, the expressed command of its Divine Author, would appear in no wise a prudent measure for removing and preventing those evils. To maintain unity and purity has always been the plausible pretence of the compilers and abettors of human systems, and we believe in many instances their sincere intention: but have they at all answered the end? Confessedly, demonstrably, they have not, no, not even in the several parties which have most strictly adopted them, much less to the catholic professing body. Instead of her catholic, constitutional unity and purity, what does the Church present us with, at this day, but a catalogue of sects and sectarian systems, each binding its respective party, by the most sacred and solemn engagements, to continue as it is to the end of the world; at least this is confessedly the case with many of them. What a sorry substitute these, for Christian unity and love! On the other hand, what a mercy is it, that no human obligation that man can come under is valid against the truth. When the Lord the healer, descends upon His people, to give them a discovery of the nature and tendency of those artificial bonds, wherewith they have suffered themselves to be bound in their dark and sleepy condition, they will no more be able to hold them in a state of sectarian bondage, than the withs and cords with which the Philistines bound Samson were able to retain him their prisoner; or, than the bonds of anti-Christ were, to hold in captivity the fathers of the Reformation. May the Lord soon open the eyes of His people to see these things in their true light, and excite them to come up out of their wilderness condition, out of this Babel of confusion, leaning upon their Beloved, and embracing each other in Him; holding fast the unity of the spirit in the bonds of peace. This gracious unity and unanimity in Jesus would afford the best external evidence of their union with Him and of their conjoint interest in the Father's love. "By this shall all men know that ye are my disciples," saith he, "if ye have love one to another." And "this is My commandment that ye love one another as I have loved you; that ye also love one another." And again, "Holy Father, keep through Thine own name, those whom Thou hast given Me that they may be one as We are," even "all that shall believe in Me, that they all may be one, as thou Father art in Me and I in Thee, that they also may be one in us; that the world may believe that Thou hast sent Me. And the glory which thou gavest Me, I have given them, that they may be one, even as we are one: I in them and Thou in Me, that they may be made perfect in Me; and that the world may know that thou hast sent Me, and hast loved them, as thou hast loved Me." May the Lord hasten it in His time. Farewell.

Peace be with all them that love our Lord Jesus Christ in sincerity. Amen.

THOS. CAMPBELL, Secretary.

THOS. ACHESON, Treasurer.

THE APPENDIX AND THE POSTSCRIPT

IN the original issue, 'the Declaration' occupied three pages, 'the Address' eighteen pages, and there was subjoined 'the Appendix' which ran to no less than thirty-one pages. Three months later a 'Postscript' of three pages was added. The 'Postscript' merely suggested two important steps to be taken to further the enterprise of The Christian Association: (1) The preparation of "a catechetical exhibition of the fulness and precision of the Holy Scriptures upon the entire subject of Christianity—an exhibition of that complete system of faith and duty expressly contained in the sacred oracles; respecting the doctrine, worship, discipline and government of the Christian Church".* This proposal must be taken in connection with the seventh proposition of 'the Address', which declared that "doctrinal exhibitions . . . be highly expedient; and the more full and explicit they be, the better",† but they must not be taken as terms of communion; (2) That a monthly magazine be published to be called *The Christian Monitor*. Neither of these projects was ever achieved.

The 'Appendix' is much more prolix in style than the rest of the document and, in these days of more terse expression, makes wearisome reading. We, therefore, have thought it better to produce a digest of this, perhaps the most important part of the whole document. Nothing is lost by leaving the 'Postscript' unpublished.

DIGEST OF THE APPENDIX

The 'Appendix' was written to explain and clarify several points in the position of the Christian Association as set forth in The Declaration and Address, more especially in the 'Address'. Dr. W. E. Garrison in his massive book, *The Disciples of Christ*, produced in conjunction with Dr. A. T. De Groot, says of it, "One principal purpose was to allay animosity by giving assurance that no campaign of proselytising was planned, and that the aim was to persuade the Churches to reform themselves."‡ The other purpose undoubtedly was—and most of the thirty-one pages are devoted to this purpose—to shew that the Christian Association did not aim at Latitudinarianism, at being doctrinally flabby. In a remarkable way the 'Appendix' shews that the writers anticipated the kind of objections which might be lodged against their document, and the kind of perversions which might easily spring from it, and which, indeed, have sprung from it.

The 'Appendix' begins by explaining that the Christian Association had no intention of interfering with "the peace and order of the settled churches"

* p. 35. The page numbers throughout refer to the original document of 1809.
† p. 16 of this edition.
‡ *The Disciples of Christ*, p. 152.

and had "no nostrum, no peculiar discovery of its own to propose to fellow-christians."* This shews that Thomas Campbell and those with him were most anxious, not to form yet another division in the Church, but rather to set up a *movement* within all the Churches. It shews, further, that, unlike many other movements which were to arise in the nineteenth century, this one propounded no peculiar doctrines upon which it wished to thrive. The writers of the document proposed nothing except the living Word of the living God as a guide to Christian faith and practice, and they emphatically trusted to the *rational* faculty in all men—that is, to common sense—to make clear the import of the revelation contained in the Bible, both as to its express declarations and as to the inferences to be drawn.

Their attitude to creeds and confessions, it is shewn, was conditioned by such confessions as that of Philadelphia, which was then most in use, especially amongst Baptists, and which is comparable with such documents as the Augsburg Confession, the Thirty-nine Articles, and the Westminster Confession. These are all Confessions compounded of abstract theological doctrines. Campbell and those with him did not have in mind such primitive creeds as that known as the Apostles' Creed, which is largely a statement of the *facts* of the Gospel, rather than theological formulations about those facts. Furthermore, they did not object to creeds as such, but to the improper use of them. "As to creeds and confessions, although we may appear to our brethren to oppose them, yet this is to be understood only *in so far* as they oppose the unity of the Church by containing sentiments not expressly revealed in the Word of God; or by the way of using them so that they become the instruments of a human or implicit faith; or oppress the weak of God's heritage. Where they are liable to none of these objections, we have nothing against them. It is the *abuse*, and not the *lawful use*, of such compilations we oppose." (See Prop. 7 of the 'Address'.)† From this it would appear that their objection to creeds and confessions was threefold: (1) Too close theological definition of articles of the Faith tended to split Christians into separate Churches; (2) Creeds and Confessions were apt to be substituted for real *personal* faith in a *personal* God. Such *intellectual* assent to theological propositions as that demanded by subscription to creeds, could be no adequate substitute for the affirmation of trust in and loyalty to the personal Lord and Redeemer, which was a total commitment of the whole person; (3) the intellectual range of Creeds and Confessions was a great barrier to 'the weak', the 'children in understanding' whom Christ came to save equally with the intellectual giants.

They further wished to draw a clear distinction between matters of 'the faith once for all delivered to the saints', which were binding upon all Christians; and matters of theological opinion which might be held within the confines of the one Church and add to its richness of life and worship, rather than imposed to split the Church into parties.

The rest of the 'Appendix' is almost exclusively devoted to repudiating the charge of Latitudinarianism. Undoubtedly the cry of 'no creed' is apt to be interpreted rather literally as 'no creed at all', that is, believe anything you like, or nothing at all. Such a charge has often been hurled against the

* p. 24. † pp. 24 and 25.

followers of Campbell. But that is a shocking caricature of their position: "After all, should any impeach us with the vague charge of Latitudinarianism (let none be startled at this gigantic term) it will prove as feeble an opponent to the glorious cause in which we, however weak and unworthy, are professedly engaged, as the Zamzummins did of old to prevent the children of Lot from taking possession of their inheritance. If we take no greater latitude than the divine law allows, either in judging persons or doctrines—either in profession, or practice (and this is the very thing we humbly propose and intend) may we not reasonably hope, that such a latitude will appear to every upright Christian perfectly innocent and unexceptionable? If this be Latitudinarianism, it must be a good thing—and therefore the more we have of it the better; and may be it is, for we are told 'the commandment is exceeding broad'; and we intend to go just as far as it will suffer us, but not one hair's breadth further—so at least says our profession."* All that they would require of members of the Church was "a manifest attachment to our Lord Jesus Christ, in faith, holiness, and charity." This was "the original criterion of Christian character—the distinguishing badge of our holy profession—the foundation and cement of Christian unity."† They were convinced that the unity of the Church did not mean a 'strict literal uniformity' in all things nor 'secure a uniformity of sentiment'. "It is granted that, in a certain degree, it would not; nor, indeed, is there anything, either in Scripture or in the nature of things, that should induce us to expect an entire unity of sentiment, in the present imperfect state. The Church may, and we believe will, come to such a Scriptural unity of faith and practice, that there will be no schism in the body; no self-preferring sect of professed and acknowledged Christians, rejecting and excluding their brethren. *This* cannot be, however, till offensive and excluding causes be removed; and everyone knows what *these* are. But that all the members should have the same identical views of all divinely revealed truths; or that there should be no difference of opinion among them, appears to us morally impossible, all things considered."‡

They claimed that the 'Address' itself was no creed, but intended only to draw attention to the "heinous nature and awful consequences of schism, and to that evil and anti-scriptural principle from which it necessarily proceeds."§ What, then, did they put in the place of creeds? Not "a vague indefinite approbation of the Holy Scriptures, as an alternative for the present practice of making the approbation of human standards a term of communion as it is undeniably evident that nothing can be further from our intention".|| Rather, they might be thought to be aiming at "too much strictness, both as to the description of character which we say ought only to be admitted, and also as to the use and application of the rule. But should this be the case, we shall cheerfully bear with it; as being fully satisfied, that not only the common sentiment of all apparently sincere, intelligent and practical Christians is on our side; but also that the plainest and most ample testimonies of the inspired volume sufficiently attest the truth and propriety of what we plead for, as essential to the scriptural unity and purity of the Christian Church; and this we humbly presume is what we should incessantly aim at. It would be strange, indeed, if in contending earnestly for the faith once for all delivered

* p. 31. † p. 36. ‡ p. 37. § p. 51. || p. 5 .

to the saints, we should overlook those fruits of righteousness—that manifest humility, piety, temperance, justice and charity—without which faith is dead, being alone. We trust we have not so learned Christ: if so be, we have been taught by Him, as the truth is in Jesus, we must have learned a very different lesson indeed."*

Rather than set up another creed—even a reformed one—they trusted to the fact that in Holy Scripture there was sufficient guidance as to what constituted the facts of the original Christian Faith and as to what defined the life and worship of the Church. It was to this that they appealed.

The 'Appendix' ends with an appeal drawn from the Missionary situation in the Mission to North American Indians on whom the divisions of the Church had had a bad effect. "Alas! poor people! how do our divisions and corruptions stand in your way? What a pity that you find us not upon original ground, such as the Apostles left the primitive churches! Had we but exhibited to you their unity and charity; their humble, honest and affectionate deportment towards each other and towards all men: you would not have had those evil and shameful things to object to our holy religion, and to prejudice your minds against it. But your conversion, it seems, awaits our reformation—awaits our return to primitive unity and love. To this may the God of mercy speedily restore us, both for your sakes and our own; that *His way* may be known upon earth, and His saving health among all nations. Let the people praise thee, O God: let all the people praise thee. Amen and amen."†

* p. 51. † p. 54.

PUBLICATIONS of THE BEREAN PRESS

COMPANION TO THE COMMUNION SERVICE.
By William Robinson, 5s.

THE SHATTERED CROSS: THE MANY CHURCHES AND THE ONE CHURCH. By William Robinson, 3s. 6d.

HOLY ORDINANCES: A MANUAL OF INSTRUCTION ON BAPTISM AND THE LORD'S SUPPER.
By William Robinson, 2s. 6d.

TOWARDS TRUE BAPTISM. By James Gray, M.A., 1s.

WHAT CHURCHES OF CHRIST STAND FOR.
By William Robinson, 1*s*.

ESSENTIALS FOR A LIVING CHURCH
By James Gray, M.A., 3s. 6d.

CHRISTIAN HYMNARY. Words Edition from 6*s*.
Tune Book. 12*s*. 6*d*.

All the above from

THE BEREAN PRESS

20 BRIGHTON ROAD, BIRMINGHAM 12